Contents

Preface

Why should you read this book?

Work-related stress is a major cause of occupational ill health, poor productivity and human error. That means increased sickness absence, high staff turnover and poor performance in your organisation and a possible increase in accidents due to human error. The Health and Safety Executive's (HSE's) Management Standards for work-related stress will help you, your employees and their representatives manage the issue sensibly and minimise the impact of work-related stress on your business. They might also help you improve how your organisation performs.

The Management Standards describe a set of conditions that reflect high levels of health, well-being and organisational performance. Following the advice in this book will enable you to identify the gap between what is happening in your organisation and these ideal conditions. It will also help you develop solutions to close this gap.

Who should use this book?

This book is aimed primarily at organisations that employ 50 or more people, but smaller businesses may also find it helpful. It is aimed at managers or staff with responsibility for managing the potential causes of work-related stress in your organisation. That might be the person who has responsibility for co-ordinating your stress risk assessment, human resources managers, health and safety officers, trade union representatives or line managers.

Although this book will be of most interest to the person taking the lead in managing the potential causes of stress, all of these groups have a role to play in the process, so they may also find it helpful.

The approach outlined here is guidance, however, following it can help you meet your legal duties.

Other resources

The CD which accompanies this book contains additional resources. You can also find up-to-date information on HSE's stress website: www.hse.gov.uk/stress.

Part 1 Introduction

'Good management is the key to managing the causes of work-related stress'

What is stress?

Stress is the adverse reaction people have to excessive pressures or other types of demand placed on them. There is a clear distinction between pressure, which can create a 'buzz' and be a motivating factor, and stress, which can occur when this pressure becomes excessive.

How big is the problem?

- About 1 in 7 people say that they find their work either very or extremely stressful (*Psychosocial working conditions in Britain in 2007*[1]).
- In 2005/06 just under half a million people in Great Britain reported experiencing work-related stress at a level they believed was making them ill.
- Depression and anxiety are the most common stress-related complaints seen by GPs, affecting 20% of the working population of the UK.
- When stress leads to absence, the average length of sick leave is 30.1 days (Labour Force Survey 2005/06[2]). This average is much higher than the average length of sick leave for work-related illness in general (21.2 days).
- A total of nearly 11 million working days were lost to stress, depression and anxiety in 2005/06.
- HSE research in 2003 into offshore work[3] found approximately 70% of common work-related stressors are also potential root causes of accidents when they were caused by human error.

What are the key reasons to manage the causes of work-related stress?

The business case 1: Costs to the business

Research has shown work-related stress to have adverse effects for organisations in terms of:

- employee commitment to work;
- staff performance and productivity;
- accidents caused by human error;
- staff turnover and intention to leave;
- attendance levels;
- staff recruitment and retention;
- customer satisfaction;
- organisational image and reputation;
- potential litigation.

It is also worth thinking about the impact that work-related stress could have on your unit or team. For example, losing one colleague for an extended period with a stress-related illness can have a dramatic impact on the workload and morale of the rest of the team.

The business case 2: Business benefits

By taking action to manage the causes of stress in your workplace, you can prevent or reduce the impact of these problems on your organisation and bring about business benefits.

Examples of this are already emerging from a number of organisations that have taken action to deal with the pressures that can cause stress at work (see case studies at the end of this section).

The moral/ethical case: Managing the causes of work-related stress prevents ill health

There is now convincing evidence that prolonged periods of stress, including work-related stress, have an adverse effect on health. Research provides strong links between stress and:

- physical effects such as heart disease, back pain, headaches, gastrointestinal disturbances or various minor illnesses; and
- psychological effects such as anxiety and depression, loss of concentration and poor decision making.

Stress can also lead to other behaviours that can have an adverse effect on psychological and physical health and well-being, for example, social withdrawal, aggressive behaviour, alcohol/drug abuse, eating disorders and working long hours.

The legal case: What the law requires

As described in more detail in Part 3, employers have duties:

- under the Management of Health and Safety at Work Regulations 1999[4] to assess the risk of stress-related ill health arising from work activities;

- under the Health and Safety at Work etc Act 1974[5] to take measures to control that risk.

HSE expects organisations to carry out a suitable and sufficient risk assessment for stress, and to take action to tackle any problems identified by that risk assessment. The Management Standards approach is guidance intended to help and encourage you to do this and to show what you have done.

Remember also that the Safety Representatives and Safety Committees Regulations 1977,[6] the Offshore Installations (Safety Representatives and Safety Committees) Regulations 1989[7] and the Health and Safety (Consultation with Employees) Regulations 1996[8] require you to consult with your employees or their representatives on any matter that affects their health or safety at work. This includes the actions you intend to take to manage the causes of work-related stress.

Case study 1

Bradford and Bingley's work on stress began with a local environmental health officer (EHO) investigation following a staff complaint. Although the investigation did not lead to formal enforcement action, the company worked with the EHO to identify an action plan for improving its arrangements for managing stress.

The company helped identify the extent of its problem using a range of analytical and anecdotal sources, mapped against the Management Standards. Analysis of these sources suggested that, while there were no systemic problems with work-related stress, there were plenty of localised issues, often centred around the Standards 'Demands' and 'Change' (see Part 2).

The company's approach to resolving this centred on the creation of a bespoke management plan for stress accompanied by training for all managers in its use. The cornerstone of the new management arrangements was a new risk assessment tool to help local managers identify potential causes of stress and identify suitable control measures.

The company's work on managing stress is seen as the start of a long-term commitment to addressing its issues in this area. However, a number of immediate interventions were possible on issues including targets, excessive working hours and organisational change.

A year on from completing the initial roll-out, the project was already showing clear business benefits: stress-related absence (measured by working hours lost) was down from its peak by 75%, saving the company £250 000 in lost wages alone. As a result the organisation has seen approximately a 1% gain in productivity for little cost.

Case study 2

Hinchingbrooke NHS Trust was experiencing an increase in stress-related illness in 2003 and the results of the NHS annual staff survey placed them in the top 20% of NHS Trusts for work pressure experienced by staff. The Trust commissioned a survey employing HSE's Management Standards Indicator Tool (see Appendix 2 and the CD). The results of this survey suggested problems with two Standards, 'Demands' and, to a lesser extent, 'Control' (see Part 2).

In response to this, in autumn 2004, the Trust introduced a six-month 'Valuing Staff' campaign. The campaign had initiatives in nine areas including:

- better training for managers;
- introducing a formula to enable them to better predict demand and match staff to that demand;
- improved communications;
- introducing a system of absence management.

The campaign had measurable results that more than paid for the action taken. For example:

- Staff sickness absence was reduced from 6% in October 2003 to 3.8% in October 2005. This meant a saving of £500 000 in the cost of agency cover.
- While sickness absence fell, the numbers of staff reporting to Occupational Health that they were suffering from stress rose, suggesting a greater awareness on the part of staff of the need to seek help before taking sick leave.
- Whereas the Trust had had a range of unfilled vacancies in 2003, by 2005 there was a waiting list of applicants who had passed their selection system. This suggested that the hospital's image as an employer had improved.
- Productivity was substantially improved. There were reductions in patient waiting times, coupled with an increase in the number of patients in the system.

Case study 3

Somerset County Council had a recognised problem with sickness absence, some of which was linked to work-related stress. The Council addressed this problem by setting up a 'Quality of Working Life' initiative in autumn 2001. This included getting key staff on board, conducting a thorough stress audit, using the results to implement interventions, and monitoring their cost and effectiveness.

The resulting reduction in sickness absence levels (from 10.75 days in 2001/02 to 7.2 days in 2004/05) represented a total net saving of approximately £1.57 million over two years.

Case study 4

Norfolk County Council employs approximately 6500 teaching staff. The Council recognised stress as a leading cause of absence and staff turnover. They successfully developed and ran a 'Well-being Programme for Schools' based on HSE's risk assessment approach to work-related stress.

The number of teachers taking time off sick due to work-related stress dropped 40% in the summer term 2005 compared with the same term in 2004.

Part 2 The Management Standards

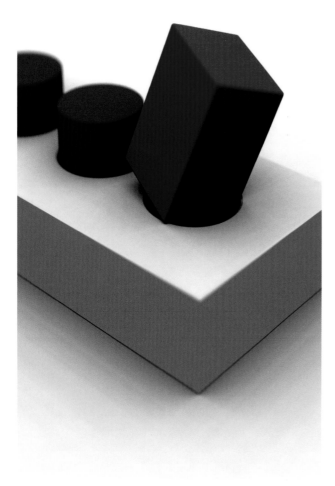

What are the Management Standards for work-related stress?

The Management Standards define the characteristics, or culture, of an organisation where the risks from work-related stress are being effectively managed and controlled.

They cover six key areas of work design that, if not properly managed, are associated with poor health and well-being, lower productivity and increased sickness absence. In other words, the six Management Standards cover the primary sources of stress at work. These are:

- **Demands** – this includes issues such as workload, work patterns and the work environment.
- **Control** – how much say the person has in the way they do their work.
- **Support** – this includes the encouragement, sponsorship and resources provided by the organisation, line management and colleagues.
- **Relationships** – this includes promoting positive working to avoid conflict and dealing with unacceptable behaviour.
- **Role** – whether people understand their role within the organisation and whether the organisation ensures they do not have conflicting roles.
- **Change** – how organisational change (large or small) is managed and communicated in the organisation.

Further information on the development and validation of the Management Standards and the evidence behind the approach is in two papers listed in the 'References' section – one describes the policy background and science[9] and the second describes the practical development.[10]

The Management Standards approach

The Management Standards approach has been developed by HSE to help reduce the levels of work-related stress reported by British workers.

The overall aim is to bring about a reduction in the number of employees who go off sick, or who cannot perform well at work because of stress. We want employers to work with employees and their representatives to implement the Management Standards by continually improving the way they manage the pressures in their workplace that can result in work-related stress. This will be good for employees and good for business.

The Management Standards approach gives managers the help they need to achieve these aims. It demonstrates good practice through risk assessment, allows evaluation of the current situation using surveys and other techniques, and promotes active discussion with employees to help decide upon practical improvements.

How can the Management Standards approach help organisations manage the pressures that can result in work-related stress?

Employers have a duty to ensure that risks arising from work activity are properly controlled.

The Management Standards approach:

- helps simplify risk assessment for work-related stress by:
  - identifying the main risk factors;
  - helping employers focus on the underlying causes and their prevention;
  - providing a step-by-step approach to carrying out a risk assessment;
- encourages employers, employees and their representatives to work in partnership to address potential sources of work-related stress throughout the organisation;
- provides a yardstick by which organisations can gauge their performance in managing the key causes of stress.

The Management Standards

In each of the Standards the 'What should be happening/States to be achieved' section defines a desirable set of conditions for organisations to work towards.

The six Management Standards are:

Demands

Includes issues like workload, work patterns, and the work environment.

The Standard is that:

- employees indicate that they are able to cope with the demands of their jobs; and
- systems are in place locally to respond to any individual concerns.

What should be happening/States to be achieved:

- the organisation provides employees with adequate and achievable demands in relation to the agreed hours of work;
- people's skills and abilities are matched to the job demands;
- jobs are designed to be within the capabilities of employees; and
- employees' concerns about their work environment are addressed.

Control

How much say the person has in the way they do their work.

The Standard is that:

- employees indicate that they are able to have a say about the way they do their work; and
- systems are in place locally to respond to any individual concerns.

What should be happening/States to be achieved:

- where possible, employees have control over their pace of work;
- employees are encouraged to use their skills and initiative to do their work;
- where possible, employees are encouraged to develop new skills to help them undertake new and challenging pieces of work;
- the organisation encourages employees to develop their skills;
- employees have a say over when breaks can be taken; and
- employees are consulted over their work patterns.

Support

Includes the encouragement, sponsorship and resources provided by the organisation, line management and colleagues.

The Standard is that:

- employees indicate that they receive adequate information and support from their colleagues and superiors; and
- systems are in place locally to respond to any individual concerns.

What should be happening/States to be achieved:

- the organisation has policies and procedures to adequately support employees;
- systems are in place to enable and encourage managers to support their staff;
- systems are in place to enable and encourage employees to support their colleagues;
- employees know what support is available and how and when to access it;
- employees know how to access the required resources to do their job; and
- employees receive regular and constructive feedback.

Relationships

Includes promoting positive working to avoid conflict and dealing with unacceptable behaviour.

The Standard is that:

- employees indicate that they are not subjected to unacceptable behaviours, eg bullying at work; and
- systems are in place locally to respond to any individual concerns.

What should be happening/States to be achieved:

- the organisation promotes positive behaviours at work to avoid conflict and ensure fairness;
- employees share information relevant to their work;
- the organisation has agreed policies and procedures to prevent or resolve unacceptable behaviour;
- systems are in place to enable and encourage managers to deal with unacceptable behaviour; and
- systems are in place to enable and encourage employees to report unacceptable behaviour.

Role

Whether people understand their role within the organisation and whether the organisation ensures that the person does not have conflicting roles.

The Standard is that:

- employees indicate that they understand their role and responsibilities; and
- systems are in place locally to respond to any individual concerns.

What should be happening/States to be achieved:

- the organisation ensures that, as far as possible, the different requirements it places upon employees are compatible;
- the organisation provides information to enable employees to understand their role and responsibilities;
- the organisation ensures that, as far as possible, the requirements it places upon employees are clear; and
- systems are in place to enable employees to raise concerns about any uncertainties or conflicts they have in their role and responsibilities.

Change

How organisational change (large or small) is managed and communicated in the organisation.

The Standard is that:

- employees indicate that the organisation engages them frequently when undergoing an organisational change; and
- systems are in place locally to respond to any individual concerns.

What should be happening/States to be achieved:

- the organisation provides employees with timely information to enable them to understand the reasons for proposed changes;
- the organisation ensures adequate employee consultation on changes and provides opportunities for employees to influence proposals;
- employees are aware of the probable impact of any changes to their jobs. If necessary, employees are given training to support any changes in their jobs;
- employees are aware of timetables for changes; and
- employees have access to relevant support during changes.

The Management Standards provide a framework for managing the risk of work-related stress and the 'States to be achieved' provide more detail. How the Management Standards and 'States to be achieved' are used in practice as part of the risk-assessment process is described in Part 4.

Part 3 Carrying out a risk assessment for work-related stress

Why assess the risks?

Under the Health and Safety at Work etc Act 1974 employers have a general duty to ensure, so far as is reasonably practicable, the health of their employees at work. This includes taking steps to make sure they do not suffer stress-related illness as a result of their work.

Regulation 3 of the Management of Health and Safety at Work Regulations 1999 requires employers to assess risks to health and safety from the hazards of work. This includes the risk of employees developing stress-related illness because of their work. You are required to carry out a 'suitable and sufficient risk assessment'.

The advice in this book will:

- help you to identify the main features of a suitable and sufficient risk assessment for work-related stress;
- provide a step-by-step guide to risk assessment based on the Management Standards approach;
- help you and your employees work together to devise an effective risk assessment for your organisation.

What does risk assessment mean?

The purpose of a risk assessment is to find out whether existing control measures preventing harm are sufficient, or if more should be done. This means that you must:

- take active steps to identify hazards (eg known stress risk factors) and related risks;
- put in place 'reasonably practicable' control measures as necessary.

Completing a risk assessment will not itself reduce work-related stress, however, the actions you take as a result should do so.

A risk assessment for work-related stress involves the same basic principles and process as a risk assessment for physical hazards. HSE recommends a step-by-step approach similar to that described in HSE's publication *Five steps to risk assessment.*[11]

Figure 1 illustrates the Management Standards step-by-step approach. Part 4 of this guidance will outline what you need to do to prepare your organisation and take you through each of the steps.

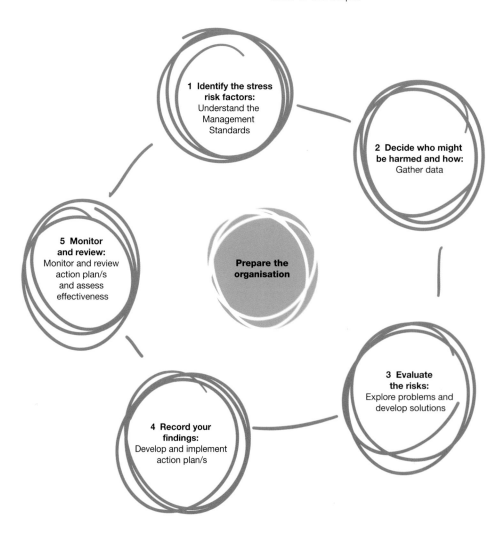

Figure 1 Management Standards step-by-step approach

Do I have to follow the Management Standards approach to risk assessment for work-related stress?

The Management Standards for work-related stress describe an approach to risk management incorporating a number of key features considered to be essential to reduce the causes of stress. If you follow this risk assessment and management process correctly, you will be adopting an approach that is considered suitable and sufficient.

Assessing your own approach

If you are starting from scratch, following the Management Standards step-by-step approach may save you time.

However, like many other organisations, you may have already developed your own approach to risk assessment for work-related stress. You may not use the word stress, for example, but may focus on positive aspects such as wellness or healthy workplaces.

The questions in the checklist opposite may help you assess what you already do. If you can answer 'yes' to all the questions, then your approach is likely to be considered a suitable and sufficient risk assessment for work-related stress.

Is my risk assessment approach suitable and sufficient?

☑ Do you include all the steps in the risk assessment process?

☑ Do you focus on prevention and organisational level solutions?

☑ Do you include provision for dealing with other issues, eg individual issues?

☑ Do you ensure commitment from all parties (senior management, employees and their representatives)?

☑ Do you have arrangements to identify those aspects of the work, work organisation or environment that are known to be risk factors for work-related stress?

☑ Does your approach highlight the extent and nature of the gap, if any, between the current situation and what is seen as good practice, eg 'the States to be achieved' in the Management Standards, for each of the identified stress risk areas?

☑ Do you involve the workforce:
- by asking about their views regarding good and bad features of workplace conditions?
- by seeking their suggestions, advice and comments on potential solutions to problems (eg improvements to working conditions, changes in the way work is organised etc)?
- by ensuring that people are empowered to contribute and feel that their views are listened to and acted on?
- by communicating outcomes (eg action plans)?

☑ Do you seek to develop and adopt solutions that are 'reasonably practicable'?

☑ Do you provide documentation to show what you have done at each stage of the process and that you are implementing the recommended actions?

It is important that you document what you have done, whether you follow the Management Standards approach or an alternative approach to carrying out a risk assessment for work-related stress. Documenting the process you have followed provides an audit trail to help you demonstrate to the relevant inspection authorities that what you have done represents a suitable and sufficient risk assessment.

Typical timescale for one complete cycle of the Management Standards risk assessment approach

It typically takes large organisations 18 months for one complete cycle of the Management Standards risk assessment approach. This includes up to six months to do the risk assessment and implement the action plan and a further 12 months to allow solutions time to have an effect and produce measurable outcomes. However, this is only a rough guide and is based mainly on the experience of larger organisations. Some solutions may show benefits much more quickly.

Experience to date suggests that 'continuous improvement' beyond the end of the first cycle will involve a much less resource-intensive approach. You should aim to integrate the Management Standards into everyday management practice and adapt them to your particular needs (rather than repeating the whole cycle).

Smaller organisations

As a smaller organisation you may find that you can use the Management Standards risk assessment approach to complete a risk assessment and implement your action plan in a much shorter time than larger organisations. For example, the activities involved in preparing the organisation and securing commitment may be much more straightforward and less time-consuming to organise.

Part 4 of this guidance will take you through each of the steps in the risk assessment approach, and, where relevant, highlight alternative approaches you may wish to adopt.

Part 4 The Management Standards step-by-step approach to risk assessment for work-related stress

Prepare the organisation

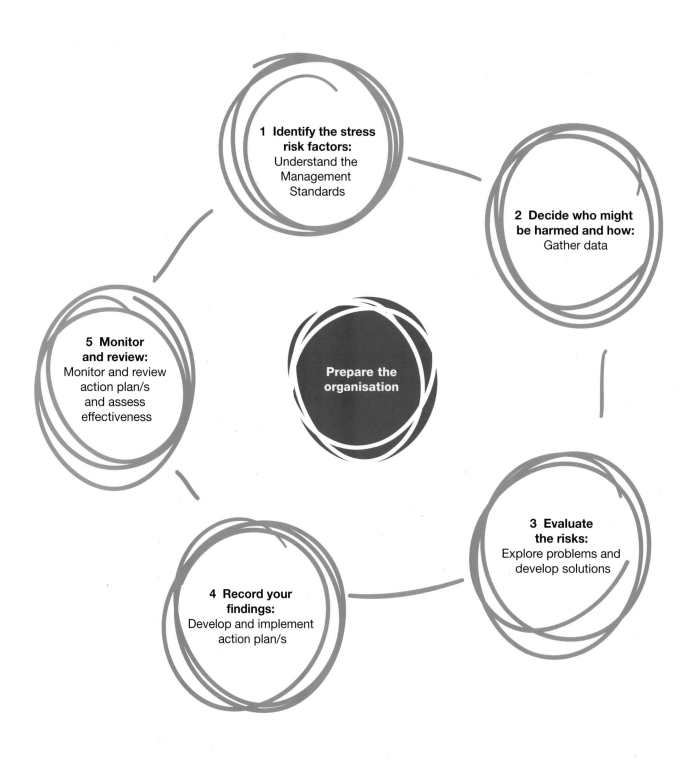

1 Identify the stress risk factors: Understand the Management Standards

2 Decide who might be harmed and how: Gather data

3 Evaluate the risks: Explore problems and develop solutions

4 Record your findings: Develop and implement action plan/s

5 Monitor and review: Monitor and review action plan/s and assess effectiveness

Prepare the organisation

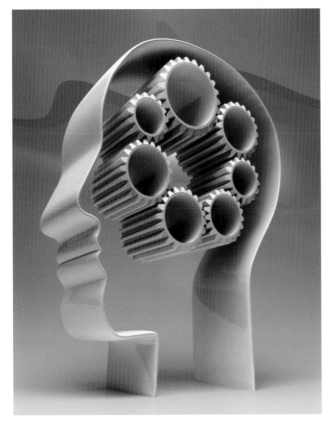

Prepare the organisation

Work to 'prepare the organisation' forms a key element of the risk assessment for work-related stress. This preparatory work is also required in other forms of risk assessment, however, it may not be seen as a separate stage in the risk assessment process. This may be because certain things are already well-established in the organisation or may not require much extra effort, for example:

- senior management commitment (to control hazards);
- relevant expertise (in hazard identification etc);
- employees' understanding of the nature of the hazards; and
- relevant organisational structures and procedures.

In the case of a risk assessment for work-related stress, this preparatory work is critical because:

- the approach is relatively new and differs from previous approaches to stress management that managers and employees may be familiar with;
- the approach relies heavily on the active participation and commitment of management, staff and specialists such as health and safety and human resources (HR) staff (with implications for both staffing and resources);
- it is likely that relevant organisational structures and procedures may need to be developed (or existing ones adapted) and sources of relevant expertise identified and/or developed;
- actions to manage the potential causes of work-related stress may affect many (if not all) parts of the organisation.

This preparatory work:

- is central to the Management Standards approach;
- may be required to introduce each step in the risk assessment process, particularly when it lasts some time or involves different staff;
- needs to be maintained over time, given the long-term commitment required by some of the actions to manage the potential causes of work-related stress.

Therefore, before you begin your risk assessment it is important that you:

- secure senior management commitment;
- secure commitment from employees and their representatives;
- set up a steering group;
- develop a project plan;
- secure adequate resources – in particular, staff time;
- develop a communications/employee engagement strategy.

Importance of senior management commitment

The Management Standards risk assessment approach depends very much on both senior management commitment and worker involvement throughout the process. Staff are only likely to take part if senior managers demonstrate their commitment to managing the causes of work-related stress.

Successfully securing senior management commitment should result in:

- senior management visibly demonstrating support and participating in communication activities;
- resources being allocated, eg extra funding or time;
- authority being delegated to relevant groups, eg a steering group.

How to secure management commitment

Many employers are already committed to managing the causes of stress at work as they recognise that this brings benefits for the organisation. If you need to get your senior managers on board, but are not sure how to do this, then you can adapt the information and examples in Part 1 to present a simple business case on these benefits. You can also make an ethical case as well as the legal case.

How to secure commitment from employees and their representatives

There are a number of ways to get employees and their representatives on board:

- Involve employee representatives (eg trade union and health and safety representatives) at the beginning of the process.

- Involve employees and their representatives in any groups you set up to take the work forward.
- If you decide to confine your efforts to a limited section of your organisation, consider how best to inform other employees.

Set up a steering group

An important step in getting started is to set up a steering group to manage and drive the process forward, with representatives from across the organisation. This can be a good way to secure senior management involvement and commitment from the start.

You will need to define exactly what the group will do and consider who will be part of it, which will lead to the clear assigning of roles and responsibilities. Within some organisations existing working groups may be able to take on some or all of these responsibilities. However, it is essential that employees are involved at every stage of the process.

Who should be part of a steering group?

Typical members of a steering group are:

- senior management;
- employee representative;
- trade union representative;
- health and safety manager;
- human resources representative;
- occupational health person;
- line management.

The membership will be determined by your individual organisational needs and structures. However, it is important to note that the Management Standards recommend a 'partnership' approach with all employee groups involved in the process. By involving all groups you increase the probability that the project will deliver real improvements and lead to a culture of change within the organisation.

What are the key activities of a steering group?

The main function of a steering group is to oversee and facilitate the Management Standards project, acting as a project management group or board. Key activities include:

- project naming;
- project management;
- planning;
- securing and managing resources;
- marketing;
- managing communications;
- monitoring progress;
- approving action plans;
- generating and approving management reports.

Key roles within the steering group

Organisations that have used the Management Standards risk assessment approach tell us that there are normally two key roles within a steering group.

The 'Project Champion':

- represents the project at board level;
- updates the board on progress;
- ensures the project is adequately resourced;
- is typically an HR Director or Facilities Director, depending on the organisational structure. These positions normally have responsibility for sickness absence and/or health and safety.

The 'Day-to-Day Champion':

- takes the role of project manager;
- organises and facilitates meetings;
- documents decisions, to provide an audit trail;
- keeps the project on schedule and on budget;
- is typically a health and safety manager or, in some cases, an occupational health or HR professional.

Following the setting up of a steering group, the project should be planned, resources allocated and communications strategies set out with details of how you will engage with staff. The CD provided with this publication includes a more detailed guide to setting up and running steering groups. You may also find it useful to look at the case studies on the CD and on the HSE website (www.hse.gov.uk/stress/experience.htm) to see how other organisations have gone about this stage of the process.

Develop a project plan

Some organisations implementing the Management Standards have experienced difficulties:

- in getting senior managers to attend steering group meetings;
- in getting people together at the same time for focus group meetings;
- in maintaining momentum, for example:
  - when there has been a long gap between the distribution of surveys and follow-up work; or
  - when resources needed to implement the Management Standards were diverted to other priorities;
- due to an underestimate of how much work was involved in implementing the Management Standards.

Some of these difficulties may have been caused by the lack of a fully developed project plan. A well-developed project plan and timeline will help you to:

- identify whose input is needed when, so that work plans can be arranged accordingly. For example, the project plan may enable senior managers to schedule steering group meetings in their diaries, and may allow managers to schedule time into their team's work plans to complete a survey or attend a focus group;
- determine whether there are any particular periods when certain activities should not take place. For example, it should help prevent you trying to run focus groups during school holidays or other periods when many people are likely to be on leave;

- maintain momentum to reduce any delay between running surveys and setting up focus groups;
- review the planning and timescales for other initiatives and help to identify any areas of potential overlap between the Management Standards approach and existing initiatives. This can reduce effort and duplication and help to integrate risk assessment for work-related stress into existing management practices.

Secure adequate resources

You need to consider:

- the staff time commitment required:
  - of the steering group members and other staff running the process;
  - of the employees involved in the process;
- the experience of staff:
  - in project management;
  - in data analysis;
  - in other approaches to consulting with staff (such as focus groups);
- finance, including any extra costs if you decide to outsource any of the work.

The experience of many organisations working through the Management Standards process is that there appear to be two pinch points with respect to resources:

- gathering data. This is the especially the case if the organisation chooses to use a staff survey. The main challenge experienced is with data entry, though this can be outsourced to a data warehousing organisation;
- staff consultation. Whatever method of consultation is chosen, it needs to be planned to ensure staff are available to participate.

Develop a communications/employee engagement strategy

You need to develop a carefully thought-through communications plan setting out recognition of the problem, and a commitment to make improvements. Two-way communications are essential to the process and to managing expectations of staff. It is important to distinguish between top-down communication (often the provision of information) and effective two-way communications.

As part of your plans for communicating with senior management you may find it useful to consider how to prepare them for possible bad news, for example, when survey results come back and they may not like what they show.

To help you ensure an effective communications process, it is important to record what you have done for each step of the process as you go along.

Stress policy

You may find it helpful to develop an organisational stress policy to show that you take the issue of work-related stress seriously and to set out what you plan to do. Appendix 1 and the CD contain an example of a stress policy.

Checkpoint

If you are following the Management Standards risk assessment approach, before you begin the next stage, you should have:

- secured senior management commitment;
- secured commitment from employees and their representatives;
- set up a steering group;
- developed a project plan;
- secured adequate resources – in particular, staff time;
- developed a communications/employee engagement strategy;
- if appropriate, developed an organisational stress policy;
- recorded what you have done.

If your organisation is following its own approach to risk assessment for work-related stress, you may still find it useful to review your coverage of all the above issues as part of your preparation before beginning your risk assessment.

Begin your risk assessment

Now you are ready to begin the step-by-step approach to assessing and managing the potential causes of work-related stress in your organisation.

Step 1 Identify the stress risk factors: Understand the Management Standards

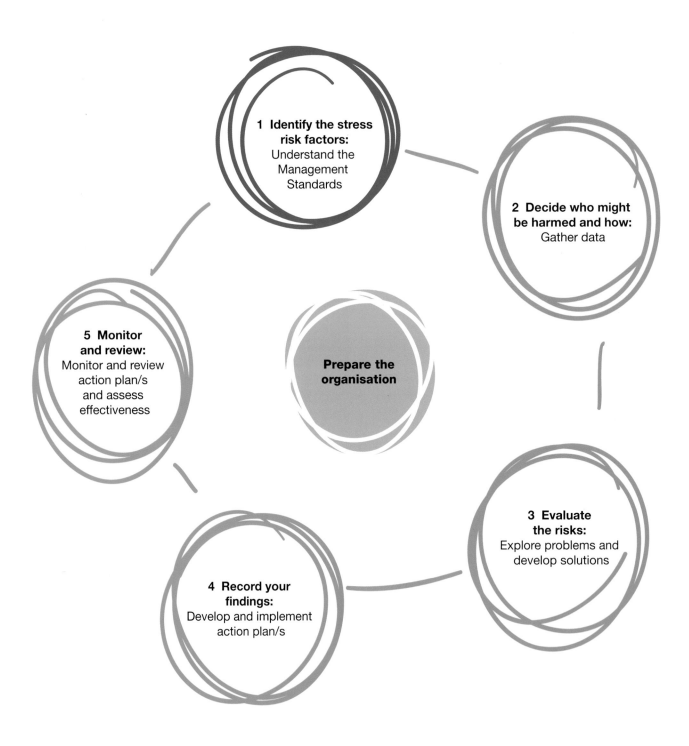

1 **Identify the stress risk factors:** Understand the Management Standards

2 **Decide who might be harmed and how:** Gather data

Prepare the organisation

3 **Evaluate the risks:** Explore problems and develop solutions

4 **Record your findings:** Develop and implement action plan/s

5 **Monitor and review:** Monitor and review action plan/s and assess effectiveness

Understand the Management Standards

The Management Standards are described in detail in Part 2 of this book. They highlight the six main risk factors for work-related stress (Demands, Control, Support, Relationships, Role and Change) and describe good management practice in each of these areas. It is important that members of the steering group and all others involved in the risk assessment process understand the Management Standards approach. This includes having a clear understanding of:

- the six broad risk factors for work-related stress on which the Management Standards are based;
- how the Management Standards translate to your organisation;
- how to compare your organisation's performance with the 'good management practice' of the Management Standards;
- risk factors for work-related stress that may be specific to your organisation or workplace;
- the need to focus on prevention and on managing the root causes of work-related stress;
- the need to focus on exploring organisational level issues.

Understand how the Management Standards translate to your organisation

The six key areas around which the Management Standards are based cover the primary sources of stress at work. So, a very useful starting point is to become familiar with these.

The six broad risk factors overlap each other to some extent, and they do not always act on their own – often they combine or interact. Try to think of the issue of 'job design' as a whole as much as you can. Avoid trying to take action on one element of work at a time – a total approach, bearing in mind the influence of the other factors, is likely to produce the best result.

There will be organisational 'hot-spots' you may wish to concentrate on, but these can best be identified by carrying out a systematic risk assessment. Your aim is to find out what are the potential causes of stress in your workplace.

If you are using the Management Standards approach, it is important to understand how they apply in, and translate to, your workplace. This includes looking at how they fit into your existing risk assessment process.

If you are not planning to use the Management Standards approach, it is important to assess whether your risk assessment approach covers all the six broad risk factors for work-related stress.

Compare your organisation's performance with the 'good management practice' of the Management Standards

The Management Standards help you measure how well you are performing in managing the potential causes of work-related stress. Each Standard provides simple statements about good management practice in each of the six areas. These include the Standard itself and, in particular, the statements of 'What should be happening/States to be achieved'.

HSE does not expect every employer to meet all the Standards at their first attempt. They represent the target for the organisation, goals that employers should be working towards through an ongoing process of risk assessment and continuous improvement. The Management Standards approach aims to help you identify where your organisation is today in terms of performance against the Management Standards and to set realistic targets for improvement.

If you are not planning to use the Management Standards approach, it is important to assess whether your risk assessment approach enables you to carry out the type of analysis described above. You may be using, or planning to use, your own key performance indicators. If so, you need to decide whether they meet these requirements.

Risk factors specific to your organisation

As well as the general stress risk factors highlighted in the Management Standards, there may be specific risks to which your employees, or some groups of your employees, may be exposed because of the nature or context of their work. You and your steering group members are well placed to identify these.

These risks may:

- fall within the six Management Standards risk factors;
- be included implicitly within the Management Standards risk factors (for example, risks due to working in contact with the public are included implicitly under Demands);
- fall outside the six Management Standards risk factors.

Whether or not you plan to use the Management Standards approach, it is important to:

- highlight these specific risks;
- assess whether your risk assessment approach enables you to address these risks; and, if not,
- put in place separate measures to enable you to assess them.

Focus on prevention and managing the root causes of work-related stress

It is important that members of your steering group and all others involved have a clear understanding of the need to focus on prevention and on managing the root causes of work-related stress, rather than trying to deal with problems only after they have occurred and people are already suffering from exposure to excessive pressures.

Focus on organisational level issues

When assessing the risks to which your employees may be exposed it is important to focus on organisational level issues that have the potential to impact on groups and possibly large numbers of employees, rather than individual employees.

Checkpoint

If you are following the Management Standards approach, before you begin the next stage you should have ensured that members of the steering group and all others involved in running the risk assessment process have a clear understanding of the Management Standards approach, including:

- the six broad risk factors for work-related stress on which the Management Standards are based;
- how the Management Standards translate to your organisation;
- how to compare your organisation's performance with the 'good management practice' of the Management Standards;
- risks for work-related stress that may be specific to your organisation or workplace;
- the need to focus on prevention and on managing the root causes of work-related stress;
- the need to focus on exploring organisational level issues.

Once you have confirmed that the steering group and all others involved in running the risk assessment process have a clear understanding of the Management Standards approach (or your own risk assessment approach), you are ready to move on to the next stage – Decide who might be harmed and how: Gather data.

Step 2 Decide who might be harmed and how: Gather data

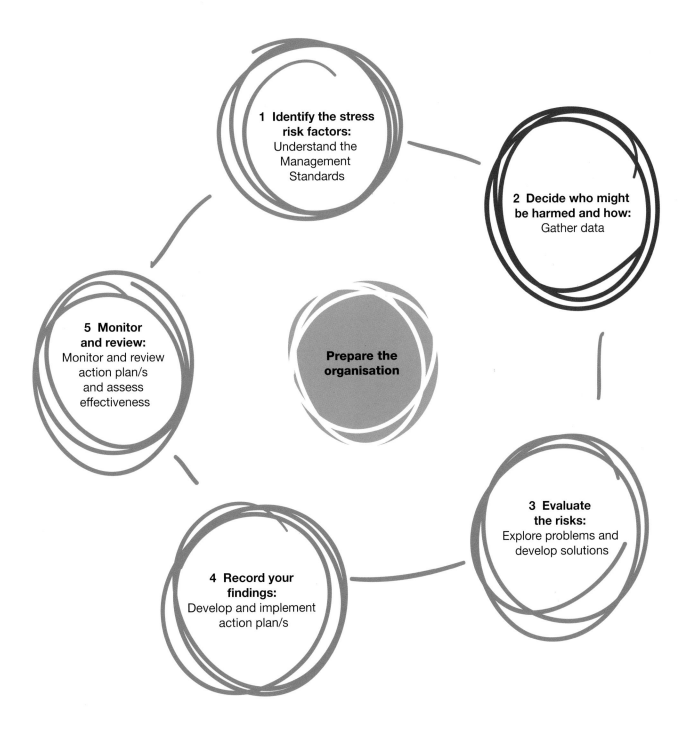

Existing sources of information or data within your organisation

Your organisation may already collect information that can be used to give an initial broad indication of whether work-related stress is likely to be a problem. This information may suggest 'hot-spots' where work-related stress is likely to be a particular problem and may also suggest what the likely underlying causes may be. Existing sources of information available to you may include those in the following paragraphs.

Sickness absence data

It is valuable to take an overview of sickness absence data in your organisation. High levels of sickness absence may indicate a potential problem area. You should investigate the reason for the absences to check whether working conditions are causing increased levels of work-related stress, which in turn is leading to sickness absence. It is worth bearing in mind that stress-related sickness absence is sometimes not reported as such, because of perceived stigma. Being open and honest within your organisation in discussing work-related stress helps to reduce this stigma and improve the reliability of the reasons staff give for absence.

Productivity data

Where productivity data indicates lower than expected performance (when compared with previous years or between different parts of the organisation), it is worthwhile examining the reasons, through discussions with employees. Working methods or conditions could be causing work-related stress and may be affecting performance.

Turnover

If your organisation, or parts of your organisation, has a higher rate of staff turnover than you would expect, this may again point to a hidden problem with work-related stress. You could think about holding 'exit interviews' to see if there are common reasons why people have decided to leave and if work-related stress was a factor. If it was, try to find out the exact cause of the problem and how you can intervene to protect your staff and prevent further losses.

Performance appraisal

Performance appraisal could offer an opportunity to have a one-to-one discussion about work and to explore whether people in your team are experiencing excessive pressure.

Team meetings

Your organisation may already hold team meetings. These can provide very useful opportunities for team members to identify and share views on current issues that may be potential sources of undue pressure. Identifying and exploring these issues during routine team meetings can help to emphasise the point that dealing with work-related stress should be an everyday part of good management practice.

Gather information or data

As a starting point for this step you need to recognise that any of your employees could be working under conditions that could cause undue pressure and so be at risk from work-related stress.

There are several different types of information or data that you can use to help you identify, in broad terms, whether work-related stress is a potential problem for your organisation and, if so, which of your employees might be likely to be harmed and how. This is the first step in assessing the gap between where you are now and where you need to be. The main sources include:

- existing sources of information or data that may already be readily available within your organisation;
- surveys;
- other ways of obtaining information about groups;
- other initiatives you are involved in.

Whether you are using the Management Standards or are adopting your own approach, it is important that you make use of the various sources of information that may be available to you.

Informal talks to staff

On a fairly regular basis, you can try to find out the mood of individuals or the team. If people seem continually unhappy, are not themselves, or are not performing well, ask if there is a problem. This can be done 'off the job', eg during regular team meetings, or 'on the job', in the form of 'walk-throughs' and 'talk-throughs'.

A walk-through is just what it says: a manager or supervisor walking through a section and observing work processes to assess whether there are any obvious aspects of the job (the way work is done, the pace of work, or working conditions etc) which may cause excessive pressure. This is most effective if done in combination with a talk-through. A talk-through involves someone describing what happens when a task is being carried out. It can be used to get employees to think about tasks in terms of the potential they have to lead to work-related stress.

Surveys

As well as the other sources mentioned, the Management Standards approach suggests using a survey as a useful source of information on whether work-related stress appears to be a potential problem for your workforce and, if so, who is likely to be affected and how.

The validity of self-report and questionnaire-based surveys is often called into question because they are dependent on how people 'feel' about issues. However, evidence suggests that individual perceptions play an important role in predicting stress-related ill health. Therefore, gathering the opinions of employees can be a useful indicator of the health of your organisation, and can form a useful part of an overall strategy to identify and address potential sources of work-related stress.

The HSE Management Standards Indicator Tool

The HSE Management Standards includes a survey tool, called the HSE Management Standards Indicator Tool (see Appendix 2 and accompanying CD), that can be distributed to all employees. It consists of 35 items that ask about 'working conditions' known to be potential causes of work-related stress. These working conditions correspond to the six stressors of the Management Standards. The employee answers according to how they feel about these aspects of their work. All responses can then be compiled into an Excel-based analysis tool, the HSE Management Standards Analysis Tool (see CD).

The HSE Management Standards Analysis Tool computes an average figure for each of the six Management Standards for your workforce, or particular part of your workforce. It gives an average result for your employees' responses for each of the six stressor areas, and these are displayed alongside a target figure. This target figure is based on the responses to a 2004 national household survey[12] in which employees assessed the performance of their organisations in managing the sources of work-related stress.

HSE suggests that your ultimate aim is for your employees' responses for each of the six stressors to be in the top 20% of the responses of employees in the national survey. If an organisation is currently not achieving that benchmark figure, then an interim figure is also given as a stepping stone towards improvement.

If you plan to use the full Management Standards survey approach

If you plan to use the full Management Standards survey approach, you can find all the relevant instructions and survey tools on the CD. These include:

- the HSE Management Standards Indicator Tool (also see Appendix 2);
- the HSE Management Standards Indicator Tool User Manual;
- the HSE Management Standards Analysis Tool. The version on the CD is current at the time of publication (and likely to remain so for some time). However, we envisage that the Analysis Tool is likely to be upgraded and improved in response to user feedback. If you plan to use these materials in the future, it will be important to check that you are using the latest version to analyse your results. The latest version can be found on HSE's Management Standards website (www.hse.gov.uk/stress/standards). You can import any results you may have from earlier versions directly into the current version;
- the HSE Management Standards Analysis Tool User Manual. This includes instructions on how to import results from earlier versions of the HSE Analysis Tool and from data generated by other survey tools.

If you plan to use the Management Standards survey tools as part of a customised 'pick and mix' approach

There are a number of ways in which you may wish to incorporate some of the Management Standards survey tools into your own customised approach. The notes accompanying the HSE Management Standards Indicator Tool in Appendix 2 and on the CD describe some of these options.

If you plan to use your own surveys

Many organisations make use of their own annual employee surveys or their own specific survey of working conditions to investigate whether work-related stress is likely to be a problem for their workforce and, if so, who is likely to be harmed and how.

If you plan to use your own survey, it is important to assess whether it covers all the relevant areas that are potential causes of stress for your workforce. One way of doing this is to assess the extent to which the questions in the survey cover each of the six Management Standard areas, eg which questions are about Demands? If there are gaps, you may need to add additional questions or you may wish to gather information about these areas in different ways, eg by discussing them with your employees.

Whether you use your own survey approach or the HSE Management Standards survey approach, the next step, communicating the results, is equally important.

How to communicate your findings

Once you have conducted the HSE work-related stress survey and processed the results using the Analysis Tool, it is important to accurately communicate the findings to the board, the workforce and their representatives.

A survey is only the start of the risk assessment process and a broad indicator of the situation in an organisation. It is intended to provide a starting point to work from in managing potential sources of work-related stress within an organisation, rather than giving a clear diagnosis of all the likely sources. The figures should be presented as a development tool for the future of the organisation, not a judgement on its past.

When the survey results indicate that the organisation has a number of areas that require action, these can form the basis of discussions with focus groups and a useful guide for future actions.

Organisations should not use survey results in isolation. Considering the results alongside information from other sources such as sickness absence data, return-to-work or exit interviews and staff appraisals should present a more informed picture.

Managers, staff representatives, trade unions and employees should be consulted and informed throughout the survey process so that the figures do not come as a shock, particularly if there is a wide variation between departments.

The CD includes more specific guidance on how to communicate the results from the HSE work-related stress survey.

Other ways of obtaining information about groups

'Toolbox talks'

In places with relatively few employees, as a starting point, it may be more appropriate to explore in small groups issues related to working conditions. You may already have arrangements in place for encouraging participation and consulting with employees. For example, routine practical talks when work is planned, sometimes referred to as 'toolbox talks', can be an opportunity to inquire about potentially stressful issues with workers. Managers can also make use of their own work planning meetings to explore potential sources of excessive pressure for themselves and their staff.

Focus groups

Focus groups can provide an opportunity to explore work-related stress issues in more depth, with more time set

aside for such discussions than may be available within standard team meetings. They also allow you to explore common issues across groups with shared interests that might not normally come together as members of teams. They allow you to explore issues in considerable depth and are particularly useful if you want to find out what specific groups of people think about their work.

The Management Standards approach suggests that focus groups are used as part of Step 3, that is, to evaluate the risk by exploring problems and developing solutions. However, none of this is written in stone and it is best to use techniques where they have proved most useful within your particular organisation.

Smaller organisations, in particular, may find it more useful to use such group approaches as part of the earlier stage of the risk assessment process.

Further information on focus groups and how to run them is available in Step 3 and in the brief guide 'How to organise and run focus groups' on the CD.

Other initiatives you are involved in

Your organisation may already be involved in other initiatives that include your own approach to gathering information on who may be harmed and how. In this case you may find it useful to integrate some parts of the Management Standards approach into your existing initiatives.

Preliminary analysis

All data and information need to be systematically collected and analysed to enable you to assess where your organisation is today in terms of performance against the desired state, as described in the Management Standards 'States to be achieved' or other benchmarks. The next step is for you or the steering group (or other relevant subgroup) to carry out a preliminary analysis on the basis of this data.

A good way of doing this is to produce a report that:

- lists all the sources of data used;
- identifies what appear to be areas of current good practice;
- identifies areas where the organisation appears to be performing less well;
- compares the **current** level of performance of your organisation in terms of 'States to be achieved' or other benchmarks with the **target state** (assesses the performance gap); then,
- identifies areas of good practice to build on;
- identifies appropriate actions to take to close the gap between the **current state** and the **target state**.

Whatever means you use to assess the risk of work-related stress, you should not rely on just one source of information, but should try to put together an overall picture by considering data from several sources. Try to avoid using questionnaires in isolation.

Checkpoint

If you are following the Management Standards approach, before you begin the next stage, you should have:

- acknowledged that work-related stress has the potential to affect any member of staff;
- considered the data available to you to indicate any potential problem areas;
- carried out a preliminary analysis comparing your performance against the Management Standards 'States to be achieved';
- identified areas of current good practice and areas where your organisation appears to be performing less well;
- recorded what you have done.

Step 3 Evaluate the risks:
Explore problems and develop solutions

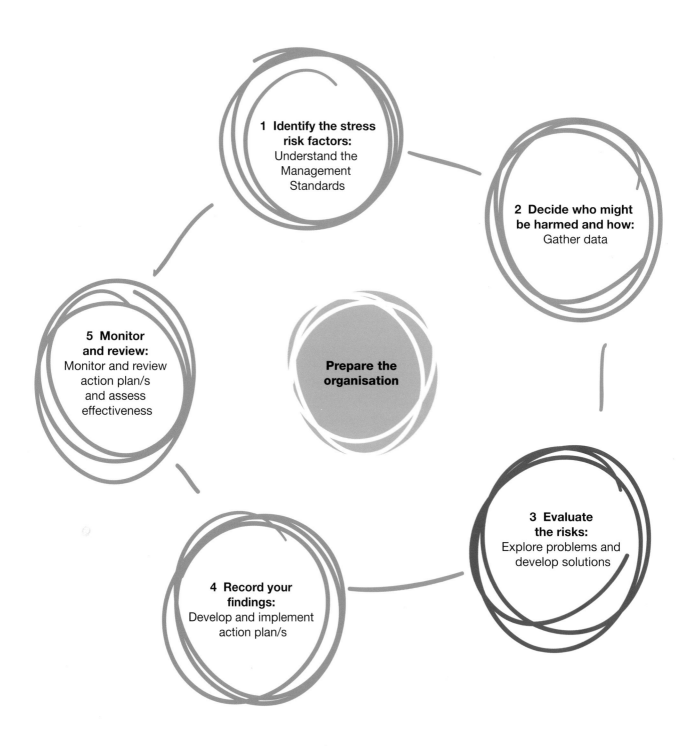

1 **Identify the stress risk factors:** Understand the Management Standards

2 **Decide who might be harmed and how:** Gather data

3 **Evaluate the risks:** Explore problems and develop solutions

4 **Record your findings:** Develop and implement action plan/s

5 **Monitor and review:** Monitor and review action plan/s and assess effectiveness

Prepare the organisation

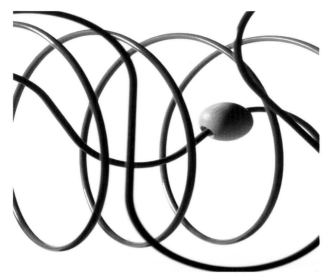

Explore problems and develop solutions

When you have collected the initial information for your risk assessment (as described in Step 2), you should confirm your findings, explore what this means locally, and discuss possible solutions using a representative sample of your workforce.

Consult employees to explore problems and confirm or challenge initial findings

It is important not to treat the initial broad picture and the gap between where you are now and where you want to be that emerge from Step 2 as definitive. You should view them as suggestions of areas that need to be confirmed, challenged or explored further with your employees and their representatives.

A useful way to consult your employees is to bring them together in 'focus groups' or discussion groups. Talking to a selection of employees with shared interests, eg from the same work group or involved in doing similar work across the organisation, will allow issues from the findings of the risk assessment to be explored in more detail. It will also provide an opportunity for you and your employees to assess the findings from the earlier stage, taking into account shared perspectives on local influences.

Experience from such focus group discussions suggests:

- issues that appear 'top of the heap' during the previous data-gathering phase may not turn out to be the most important issues for your employees;
- even when the data appear to suggest clear hot-spots, it is important to check this out with your employees;
- new issues often emerge during these group discussions. This may reflect more recent changes in working conditions (eg as a result of organisational change). However, it can also be because group techniques such as focus groups allow employees to discuss, analyse and articulate issues in ways that they may not previously have had the opportunity to do.

Link problems to solutions using focus groups

Focus groups, or similar discussion groups, allow you to explore and confirm with your employees the main potential sources of excessive pressure in the workplace. They also provide an ideal opportunity to discuss possible solutions.

It is critical that your employees and their representatives participate in this process as:

- they are often closest to the issues identified;
- they can be invaluable sources of knowledge of what will work and what will not work in practice;
- employees who have taken an active part in developing and agreeing solutions as members of such a group are more likely to help ensure the success of any agreed actions.

HSE's experience suggests that groups of between six and ten people work best. This is particularly true where the topics are likely to be sensitive or complex and you are looking to move on to develop solutions. The numbers of your employees involved in this stage will depend on the size of your organisation and local circumstances.

During the focus group or discussion group, you may find it useful to consider the 'States to be achieved' of the Management Standards, and whether this good practice is actually happening in your organisation. You may find that this can help provide structure to some of your discussions.

For further information on setting up and running focus groups see 'How to organise and run focus groups' on the CD.

You may have developed your own approaches to consultation with staff and their representatives and choose not to use focus groups. What is important, however, is that all stakeholders (management, employees and their representatives) are represented in any consultation process and have a route into any forum used.

How to develop solutions

The process of developing solutions is often seen as the most difficult part of managing the possible causes of work-related stress. The ideal to aim for is the development of locally developed solutions that take into account the particular context of your workplace.

This section contains some suggestions in the form of prompts on how to develop solutions. The CD contains some case studies that provide examples of what other organisations have done to successfully deal with problematic working conditions. New case studies are also regularly added to the HSE website.

You may find that these could help you and your employees as you work through the process. The idea is not to offer pre-packaged 'off-the-shelf' solutions, but rather to offer a resource you can use to develop your own solutions.

Prompts to solutions

When talking about work-related stress it may help to remember the following:

- Make sure enough time is spent clarifying what the problem is. It is important to be as specific as possible as this will help you develop effective solutions.
- Ask how this area of work activity became a problem. What happened? Has it always been a problem? If not, what has changed?
- What would be the mechanisms for introducing suggested improvements? Who will take the work forward? Who needs to be involved? What are the first steps? How will you monitor progress?
- Is the problem a one-off? Is any action really required? If it is, how will suggested solutions solve identified problems?
- Finally, it is important not to take on too many actions. You may need to prioritise.

Some things to consider if you have identified a problem with Demands

Possible solutions

Workload

- Develop personal work plans to ensure staff know what their job involves.
- Hold weekly team meetings to discuss the anticipated workload for the forthcoming week (and to deal with any planned absences).
- Hold monthly meetings with individuals to discuss their workload and any anticipated challenges.
- Adjust work patterns to cope with peaks and staff absences (this needs to be fair and agreed with employees).
- Ensure sufficient resources are available for staff to be able to do their jobs (time, equipment etc).
- Provide training (formal or informal) to help staff prioritise, or information on how they can seek help if they have conflicting priorities.

Competency

- Devise a system to keep training records up to date to ensure employees are competent and comfortable in undertaking the core functions of their job.
- Consider implementing personal development/training plans which require individuals to identify development/training opportunities which can then be discussed with management.
- Link training to performance monitoring arrangements to ensure it is effective and sufficient.

Working patterns

- Review working hours and shift work systems – have these been agreed with staff?
- Consider changes to start and end times to help employees to cope with pressures external to the organisation (eg child care, poor commuting routes etc).
- Develop a system to notify employees of unplanned tight deadlines and any exceptional need to work long hours.

Physical environment and violence

- Ensure your risk assessments for physical hazards and risks are up to date.
- Assess the risk of physical violence and verbal abuse. Take steps to deal with this in consultation with employees and others who can help (eg the police, charities).
- Provide training to help staff deal with and defuse difficult situations (eg difficult phone calls, aggressive members of the public).

Do . . .

- Allow regular breaks, especially when the work is complex or emotionally demanding.
- Provide realistic deadlines.
- Provide adequate training and resources for doing the job.
- Design jobs that provide stimulation and opportunities for workers to use their skills.
- Provide sufficient challenge/pressure to keep staff motivated and interested in their work.
- Attend to the physical environment – take steps to reduce unwanted distraction, disturbance, noise levels, vibration, dust etc where possible.
- Assess the risk of physical violence and verbal abuse, and take steps to deal with it.

Don't . . .

- Ask people to do tasks that they are not trained to do.
- Encourage staff to take work home with them.
- Allocate more work to a person or team unless they have the resources to cope with it.
- Allow workers to 'cope' by working longer hours.
- Ask young people (under 18 years of age) to take on work that may be beyond their emotional maturity.

Some things to consider if you have identified a problem with Control

Possible solutions

- Agree systems that enable staff to have a say over the way their work is organised and undertaken, eg through project meetings, one-to-ones, performance reviews.
- Hold regular discussion forums during the planning stage of projects to talk about the anticipated output and methods of working. Provide opportunities for discussion and input.
- Allocate responsibility to teams rather than individuals to take projects forward:
  - discuss and define teams at the start of a project;
  - agree objectives;
  - agree roles;
  - agree timescales;
  - agree the provision of managerial support, eg through regular progress meetings.

- Talk about the way decisions are made – is there scope for more involvement?
- Talk about the skills people have and if they believe they are able to use these to good effect. How else would they like to use their skills?

Do . . .

- Allow staff some control over the pace of their work.
- Allow and encourage staff to participate in decision-making.
- Empower people to make decisions about the way they work.
- Negotiate shift-work schedules.

Don't . . .

- Monitor employees' movements in detail (including breaks).
- Monitor working style, unless necessary (eg where there are child protection needs).
- Ask staff to stay late without notice.

Some things to consider if you have identified a problem with Support

Possible solutions

- Hold regular one-to-one meetings to talk about any emerging issues or pressures.
- Hold regular liaison/team meetings to discuss unit pressures.
- Include 'work-related stress/emerging pressures' as a standing item for staff meetings and/or performance reviews.
- Seek examples of how people would like to, or have, received good support from managers or colleagues – can these be adopted across the unit?
- Ask how employees would like to access managerial support, eg 'open door' policies, or agreed times when managers are able to discuss emerging pressures.
- Introduce flexibility in work schedules (where possible) to enable staff to cope with domestic commitments.
- Develop training arrangements and refresher sessions to ensure training and competencies are up to date and appropriate for the core functions of employees' jobs.
- Talk about ways the organisation could provide support if someone is experiencing problems outside work.
- Disseminate information on other areas of support (human resources department, occupational health, trained counsellors, charities).
- Offer training in basic counselling skills/access to counsellors.

Do . . .

- Ensure staff receive sufficient training to undertake the core functions of their job.
- Provide constructive, supportive advice at annual appraisal.
- Provide flexibility in work schedules, where possible.
- Allow phased return to work after long-term sickness absence.

- Hold regular liaison/team meetings.
- Provide opportunities for career development.
- Deal sensitively with staff experiencing problems outside work.

Don't . . .

- Trivialise the problems of others.
- Discriminate against people on grounds of sex, race or disability or any other reason.

Some things to consider if you have identified a problem with Relationships

Possible solutions

- Develop a written policy for dealing with unacceptable behaviour at work – communicate this to staff.
- Agree and implement procedures to prevent, or quickly resolve, conflict at work – communicate this to staff.
- Agree and implement a confidential reporting system to enable the reporting of unacceptable behaviour.
- Agree and implement a grievance and disciplinary procedure for dealing with unacceptable behaviour – circulate and/or display these.
- Select or build teams which have the right blend of expertise and experience for new projects.
- Provide training to help staff deal with and defuse difficult situations.
- Encourage good communication and provide appropriate training to aid skill development (eg listening skills, confidence building etc).
- Discuss how individuals work together and how they can build positive relationships.
- Identify ways to celebrate success (eg informal lunches/wash-up meetings at the end of a project).

Do . . .

- Encourage good, honest, open communication at all levels in work teams.
- Provide opportunities for social interactions among workers.
- Provide support for staff who work in isolation.
- Create a culture where colleagues trust and encourage each other.
- Agree which behaviours are unacceptable and ensure people are aware of these.

Don't . . .

- Allow any bullying behaviour or harassment.

Some things to consider if you have identified a problem with Role

Possible solutions

- Hold team meetings to enable members to clarify their role and to discuss any possible role conflict.
- Display team/department targets and objectives to help clarify unit and individual role.

- Agree specific standards of performance for jobs and individual tasks and review periodically.
- Introduce personal work plans which are aligned to the outputs of the unit.
- Introduce or revise job descriptions to help ensure the core functions and priorities of the post are clear.
- Hold regular one-to-one meetings to ensure individuals are clear about their role and know what is planned for the coming months.
- Develop suitable induction arrangements for new staff – make sure all members of the team understand the role and responsibilities of the new recruit.

Do . . .

- Provide a clear job description.
- Define work structures clearly, so that all team members know who is doing what, and why.
- Give all new members of staff a thorough induction to your organisation.
- Define work objectives (eg through a personal work plan).
- Avoid competing demands, such as situations where it is difficult to meet the needs of the business and the customer.

Don't . . .

- Make changes to the scope of someone's job, or their responsibilities (eg at promotion) without making sure that the individual knows what is required of them, and accepts it.

Some things to consider if you have identified a problem with Change

Possible solutions

- Ensure all staff are aware of why the change is happening – agree a system for doing this.
- Define and explain the key steps of the change. Ensure employee consultation and support is a key element of the programme.
- Establish a system to communicate new developments quickly.
- Agree methods of communication (eg meetings, notice boards, letters, e-mail, feedback forums etc) and frequency (eg weekly, monthly).
- Ensure staff are aware of the impact of the change on their jobs.
- Provide a system to enable staff to comment and ask questions before, during and after the change. Have an 'open door' policy to help staff who want to talk to their managers about their concerns. Involve staff in discussions about how jobs might be developed and changed.
- Review unit and individual work plans after the change to ensure unit and individual objectives are clear.

Do . . .

- Explain what the organisation wants to achieve and why it is essential that the change(s) takes place.

- Consult staff at an early stage, and throughout the change process.
- Involve staff in the planning process so that they understand how their work fits in.

Don't . . .

- Delay communicating new developments.
- Underestimate the effects of minor changes.

Develop focus group action plan/s

The overall aim of each focus group, or similar forum, is to explore problems and to begin the process of developing solutions. The Management Standards approach suggests that a key output from the focus group would be a proposed or preliminary action plan, containing suggestions and recommendations for action at different levels of the organisation. For example, this might contain:

- suggestions for actions the organisation as a whole needs to take, or issues it needs to address;
- suggestions for actions the Department/Division or Section of the organisation needs to take, or issues it needs to address;
- if the focus group is team based, actions the team agrees need to be taken forward and has within its power to influence.

Since there are likely to be a number of different preliminary action plans produced by different focus groups, it is likely that these will have to be reviewed and turned into an action plan for the organisation (see Step 4).

Communicate the results: Provide feedback

It is important that you communicate with management, employees and their representatives. You should keep them updated as you go through this process. For example, it is unrealistic to expect employees to participate in focus groups to discuss problems without a commitment to at least share the outcome with them soon afterwards.

Checkpoint

If you are following the Management Standards approach, before you begin the next stage, you should have:

- consulted employees to discuss problem areas in more detail;
- worked in partnership with employees and their representatives to develop actions to take;
- ensured that issues affecting individuals are addressed;
- fed back results to managers, employees and employee representatives, with a commitment to follow-up;
- recorded what you have done.

Step 4 Record your findings: Develop and implement action plan/s

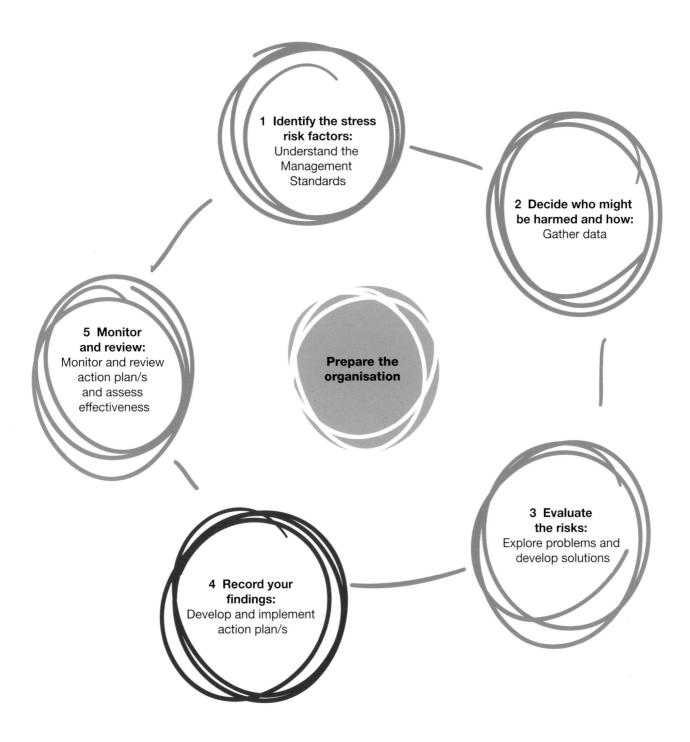

1 **Identify the stress risk factors:** Understand the Management Standards

2 **Decide who might be harmed and how:** Gather data

3 **Evaluate the risks:** Explore problems and develop solutions

4 **Record your findings:** Develop and implement action plan/s

5 **Monitor and review:** Monitor and review action plan/s and assess effectiveness

Prepare the organisation

Action plans

By this stage in the Management Standards risk assessment approach you will have consulted your employees, explored areas of concern and taken some initial steps to develop some proposed solutions. It is important that you record your findings. The Management Standards approach suggests that the best method of achieving this is to produce and disseminate an action plan. An action plan will:

- help you set goals to work towards;
- help you to prioritise;
- demonstrate that you are serious about addressing employees' concerns;
- provide you with something to evaluate and review against.

Develop your action plan/s

Preliminary action plans

The Management Standards approach suggests that a key output from each of the focus groups, or other discussion groups, should be a preliminary action plan. In developing these action plans it is useful to try to bundle together actions into:

- strategic, organisational actions that they wish to flag up to the steering group;
- actions that members of the focus group may be able to influence and take forward within their team/unit.

Overall action plan

The Management Standards approach suggests that the steering group should be responsible for collating the relevant sections of the various preliminary action plans into an overall action plan for the organisation, or part of the organisation. It is likely that the steering group will want to focus on the strategic, organisational actions in developing an overall action plan, though you may find it useful to have sections aimed at different levels of the organisation depending on the nature of your organisation and the problems you have identified.

Whether you are using the Management Standards or an alternative approach to risk assessment, action plans are a key part of your risk assessment and should at least include the following:

- what the problem is;
- how the problem was identified;
- what you are going to do in response;
- how you arrived at this solution;
- some key milestones and dates for them to be reached;
- a commitment to provide feedback to employees on progress;
- a date for reviewing against the plan.

When formulating your action plans it is important to ensure that the actions suggested:

- are given an order of priority;
- have sufficient resources allocated to them;
- are assigned to an individual or function; and
- have an agreed timescale for completion.

You might find it useful to make use of the **SMART** (**S**pecific, **M**easurable, **A**greed, **R**ealistic and **T**ime bound) acronym.

There is no prescribed method or format for an action plan. However, Appendix 3 and the CD include a template and worked example that you may want to use. The action plan needs to be agreed with employees, senior management and employee representatives. The final plan should be shared with employees.

Implement your action plan/s

To realise any benefits, the agreed and approved overall action plan and any lower level plans should be implemented as planned. Depending on the level of the plans, eg board, department or team, actions may be implemented at the appropriate levels within the organisation. Procedures should be in place to record actions taken, plans developed and to measure and evaluate the effectiveness of specific actions (see Step 5).

Checkpoint

Before you begin the next stage, you should have:

- created and agreed with senior management, employees and their representatives an overall action plan for the implementation of solutions;
- shared your action plan with all employees, including dates for monitoring and review;
- begun the process of implementing the action plan and any lower level plans;
- recorded actions taken.

Step 5 Monitor and review: Monitor and review action plan/s and assess effectiveness

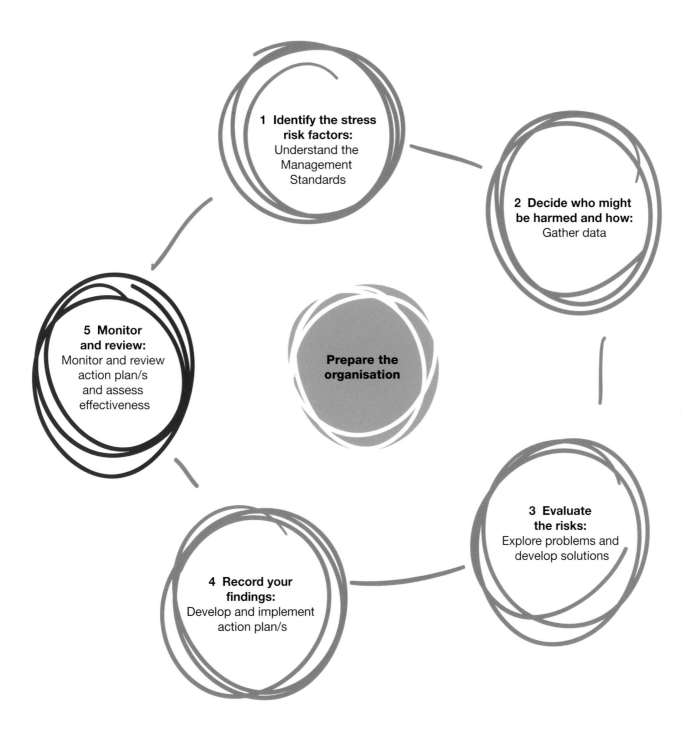

1 **Identify the stress risk factors:** Understand the Management Standards

2 **Decide who might be harmed and how:** Gather data

Prepare the organisation

3 **Evaluate the risks:** Explore problems and develop solutions

4 **Record your findings:** Develop and implement action plan/s

5 **Monitor and review:** Monitor and review action plan/s and assess effectiveness

How to review your work

It is essential that you review any action you take to tackle the sources of excessive workplace pressure. You need to:

- monitor against your action plan to ensure the agreed actions are taking place;
- evaluate the effectiveness of the solutions you implement;
- decide what further action or data gathering, if any, is needed.

Monitor and record progress against your action plan

Periodically check that agreed actions are being undertaken, for example, that meetings are being held, or that there is evidence that certain activities have taken place. It is important to make a record of this progress against your action plan.

Evaluate the effectiveness of solutions

Timescale

The timescale within which you evaluate any solutions will depend on what kind of solutions you have developed. How long actions take to deliver their expected 'measurable' outcomes can vary greatly. It is likely some will be aimed at quick-wins. For example, something simple like an adjustment to the physical environment could take only days. It could take months to pilot a complicated long-term solution (such as a new rostering system) and much longer still for something aimed at delivering long-term culture change.

The timing of your reviews will depend on how long it will take to implement each action and how long the focus group and the steering group expect it will take to have any impact.

Methods of gathering information and data

The methods of gathering information and data to evaluate the effectiveness of solutions will again depend on the kind of solutions you have developed.

Ask your employees

It is important to ask those involved whether they feel the solutions are having the desired effect. You may decide you only need to speak to a sample of those involved. Alternatively, you may feel it is important to ensure that the solutions are working for everybody.

You may find it useful to use a mixture of approaches to consult staff, for example:

- set up specific meetings to review progress on major actions;
- set up regular sessions to talk with your staff about sources of work-related pressure, for example, as part of team meetings;
- make use of informal contacts with staff to ask about the effectiveness of solutions.

Gather data

Another way to demonstrate the effectiveness of your plan is to collect data on such things as employee turnover, sickness absence and productivity, and to measure progress against emerging trends or changes in this data.

Follow-up surveys

One way to measure progress is to repeat the Management Standards survey or other survey you may have used as part of Step 2. The Management Standards approach suggests that you do this after a period of time as part of the 'continuous improvement' model. You may wish to set this up as an annual survey or as part of an annual survey.

Checkpoint

As part of Step 5 you should have:

- monitored against your action plans to ensure that agreed actions are taking place;
- evaluated the effectiveness of the solutions you implemented;
- decided what further action or data gathering, if any, is needed.

You have now completed all the steps in the HSE Management Standards risk assessment approach. While the main focus of your risk assessment will have been on issues that are likely to be potential sources of stress for groups of your employees, you should check that you have also dealt with individual concerns.

Part 5 Deal with individual concerns

Individual concerns

The main focus of the Management Standards risk assessment approach described in the previous sections is on issues that are likely to be potential sources of stress for groups of your employees.

The surveys and focus groups may identify that some individuals are experiencing problems that the majority of employees are not. The solutions you develop for the majority of your employees may not address these problems. However, you still have a duty of care to protect the health and well-being of these individuals too.

It is essential that you develop ways for employees to raise their concerns. These could include the following:

- create an environment where employees are encouraged to talk, both formally and informally, to their manager or another person in their management chain;
- remind employees that they can speak to trade union representatives, health and safety representatives, or human resources personnel;
- encourage employees to talk to someone in the organisation or seek advice from occupational health advisors, or their GP if they are concerned about their health;
- introduce mentoring and other forms of co-worker support;
- provide employee assistance (counselling) services.

How do I react to employee concerns?

Possibly the most critical 'take-home message' to come out of recent civil claims for compensation for suffering work-related stress is that where stress is 'foreseeable', action must be taken to limit the problem. So what should the line manager do when an employee reports that they are under excessive pressure or feeling stressed?

While it is not expected that line managers be experts on stress, it is expected that they should be able to do enough to generate action towards limiting the harm to the individual, when it is directly drawn to their attention.

At the organisational level it should be clear who has the responsibility to progress the report or complaint of work-related stress.

Suggested actions

- First of all it is important to speak to the person involved, to find out what has led to the complaint, and what can be done about it. This should not be unduly delayed, although in some cases it may be necessary to include other people who might be involved in the issue in a formal meeting. Always take complaints seriously, and ensure that the employee is not fobbed off, or belittled in any way.
- Where the distress is serious, fault is cited, and things have clearly gone beyond what the line manager can deal with, ask for expert assistance.
- When the complaint involves relationship issues with the line manager, or other team members, it is very useful to involve human resources, occupational health and a representative for the employee when working through the problem.
- Where it is possible to identify a clearly work-related problem, it is essential to rectify the situation as swiftly as possible, even if this involves compromise on either side. It is much easier to intervene successfully when the employee remains at work, than after they have gone off sick.
- Follow this with a wider formal appraisal of the working conditions in the relevant area, which should include other employees and, where appropriate, their representatives. This should be documented. The risks of stress should be controlled, and an action plan agreed.
- Even where 'home' influences are impacting on the employee's performance and perceptions of their work (eg care-giving responsibilities limiting work hours/energy levels), and this is a major contribution to the complaint, it is generally in the employer's interest to support the employee, rather than dismiss the problem as irrelevant to the business. If an employee is not working well, for whatever underlying reason, it will impact on their performance at work and may also affect their colleagues.
- Some organisations have found it helpful to use the Management Standards to structure discussions with individuals who are known to be vulnerable to stress or who are potentially vulnerable.

How do I deal with home-related stress?

People do bring home-related stress into the workplace. Although you are not legally responsible for stress that originates in the home, well-managed organisations will have arrangements that allow them to address this. This might include such things as access to counselling services, adaptations to the work or changes to working hours.

Managers often say it is difficult to identify what stress is caused by problems at home and what is caused by work. Using the Management Standards can help to tease this out.

A more detailed discussion on individual issues, eg home-related stress, is beyond the scope of the current guidance. For more information see 'Useful resources'.

Part 6 What to do next:
What do I do after I have completed
all the steps and addressed any
individual issues?

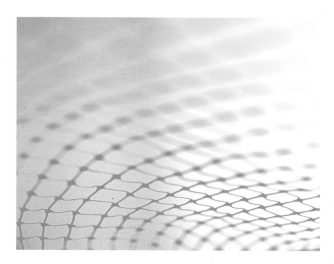

Review your organisation's policies and procedures

Part 4 (Step 4) explained action planning and how typically the actions generated by the focus groups will fall into different categories based on the different levels in your organisation (eg board, department or team). These actions will address the gaps between current organisational performance and that described in the Management Standards 'States to be achieved'. However, it is also useful to consider the reasons behind these gaps in performance and examine whether your organisation's policies and procedures need to be reviewed in the light of the findings from your risk assessment.

It is often the case that policies and procedures do not adequately reflect the current ways of working, due to the continuous change that organisations experience. This can increase the pressure experienced by employees. The Management Standards approach can help this process of organisational learning by providing your organisation with a framework to work with employees to address the gaps in your current performance.

The experience of Bradford and Bingley highlights what organisations can learn from the outcome of the risk assessment process that can inform other areas of their business and related policies and procedures.

'. . . Furthermore the messages contained in the stress management training have been reinforced by a new culture and values programme being rolled out across the company, and the delivery of stress management, along with general health and safety management training, has been incorporated into the company's training academy.

This is no "t-shirt and mouse mat" exercise, it will need continued attention in the future so it becomes "the way we do it at B&B".'

John Hamilton, Head of Group Health and Safety

(see CD for full Bradford and Bingley case study).

Make the Management Standards part of everyday management

The Management Standards are concerned with the prevention and management of common health problems and the drive towards good jobs to enhance the performance of your organisation.

The Management Standards approach, as with any risk assessment, should be concerned with making steady improvements in the way you manage risks to your organisation's performance. It is critical that you are committed to continuously working with employees to identify and address the problems in your workplace that could lead to their ill health and adversely affect the performance of your organisation.

Since the process is continuous, it is envisaged that the evaluation and monitoring activities in Part 4 (Step 5) will merge naturally into everyday management.

Whether you use the Management Standards approach or an alternative approach to risk assessment, it is important that this is seen as part of the normal day-to-day activities of your line managers, and is integrated into their role as far as possible.

Identify and develop the competencies your managers need to manage potential sources of work-related stress

To help this process of integration, HSE recently commissioned research to identify and develop the management behaviours associated with the effective management of potential sources of work-related stress. The research produced a framework ('Managing stress at work: A competency framework for line managers' – see Appendix 4) that was mapped onto the six Management Standards areas and onto other frameworks of general management competencies.

The findings from this research indicate that there is considerable overlap between the management competencies required for preventing and reducing potential sources of stress at work and general management competencies. This supports the central message of this guidance that good management is the key to managing the causes of work-related stress.

Appendices

Appendix 1: Example of a stress policy

Introduction

We are committed to protecting the health, safety and welfare of our employees. We recognise that workplace stress is a health and safety issue and acknowledge the importance of identifying and reducing workplace stressors.

This policy will apply to everyone in the company. Managers are responsible for implementation and the company is responsible for providing the necessary resources.

Definition of stress

The Health and Safety Executive defines stress as 'the adverse reaction people have to excessive pressure or other types of demand placed on them'. This makes an important distinction between pressure, which can be a positive state if managed correctly, and stress which can be detrimental to health.

Policy

- The company will identify all workplace stressors and conduct risk assessments to eliminate stress or control the risks from stress. These risk assessments will be regularly reviewed.
- The company will consult with Trade Union Safety Representatives on all proposed action relating to the prevention of workplace stress.
- The company will provide training for all managers and supervisory staff in good management practices.
- The company will provide confidential counselling for staff affected by stress caused by either work or external factors.
- The company will provide adequate resources to enable managers to implement the company's agreed stress management strategy.

Responsibilities

Managers

- Conduct and implement recommendations of risks assessments within their jurisdiction.
- Ensure good communication between management and staff, particularly where there are organisational and procedural changes.
- Ensure staff are fully trained to discharge their duties.
- Ensure staff are provided with meaningful developmental opportunities.
- Monitor workloads to ensure that people are not overloaded.
- Monitor working hours and overtime to ensure that staff are not overworking. Monitor holidays to ensure that staff are taking their full entitlement.
- Attend training as requested in good management practice and health and safety.
- Ensure that bullying and harassment is not tolerated within their jurisdiction.
- Be vigilant and offer additional support to a member of staff who is experiencing stress outside work, eg bereavement or separation.

Occupational health and safety staff

- Provide specialist advice and awareness training on stress.
- Train and support managers in implementing stress risk assessments.
- Support individuals who have been off sick with stress and advise them and their management on a planned return to work.
- Refer to workplace counsellors or specialist agencies as required.
- Monitor and review the effectiveness of measures to reduce stress.
- Inform the employer and the health and safety committee of any changes and developments in the field of stress at work.

Human resources

- Give guidance to managers on the stress policy.
- Help monitor the effectiveness of measures to address stress by collating sickness absence statistics.
- Advise managers and individuals on training requirements.
- Provide continuing support to managers and individuals in a changing environment and encourage referral to occupational workplace counsellors where appropriate.

Employees

- Raise issues of concern with your safety representative, line manager or occupational health.
- Accept opportunities for counselling when recommended.

Safety representatives

- Safety representatives must be meaningfully consulted on any changes to work practices or work design that could precipitate stress.
- Safety representatives must be able to consult with members on the issue of stress including conducting any workplace surveys.
- Safety representatives must be meaningfully involved in the risk assessment process.
- Safety representatives should be allowed access to collective and anonymous data from HR.
- Safety representatives should be provided with paid time away from normal duties to attend any Trade Union training relating to workplace stress.
- Safety representatives should conduct joint inspections of the workplace at least every three months to ensure that environmental stressors are properly controlled.

Safety Committee

- The joint Safety Committee will perform a pivotal role in ensuring that this policy is implemented.
- The Safety Committee will oversee monitoring of the efficacy of the policy and other measures to reduce stress and promote workplace health and safety.

Signed by

Managing Director:
Date:

Employee Representative:
Date:

Appendix 2: The HSE Management Standards Indicator Tool

Notes on the HSE Management Standards Indicator Tool

The HSE Management Standards Indicator Tool is also available in a convenient printable form on the CD, together with a copy of the HSE Management Standards Indicator Tool User Manual. It is also available in a number of different languages on HSE's Management Standards website (www.hse.gov.uk/stress/standards).

If you plan to use the HSE Management Standards Indicator Tool as part of a customised 'pick and mix' approach

There are a number of ways in which you may wish to incorporate some of the Management Standards survey tools into your own customised approach, for example:

- **Incorporating the HSE Management Standards Indicator Tool into your own survey:** You may wish to incorporate the HSE Management Standards Indicator Tool into your own survey. In this case, we would suggest that you keep the question wording and scoring system the same and the items in the same order and use the HSE Management Standards Analysis Tool to analyse your results. This will enable you to compare your results with the HSE benchmark data. If you use other software to carry out a preliminary analysis of the data, please note that the scoring system is reversed for some items.
- **Using online survey tools:** You may wish to use the HSE Management Standards Indicator Tool in conjunction with a commercially available survey tool to conduct an online survey. Once you have completed the survey you can use the import facility to import your results directly into the HSE Management Standards Analysis Tool. Appendix C of the HSE Management Standards Analysis Tool User Manual describes the CSV format requirements for users wishing to export data from other software applications in a format suitable for import into the Analysis Tool.

Instructions

It is recognised that working conditions affect worker well-being. Your responses to the questions below will help us determine our working conditions now, and enable us to monitor future improvements. In order for us to compare the current situation with past or future situations, it is important that your responses reflect your work in the last six months.

		Never	Seldom	Sometimes	Often	Always
1	I am clear what is expected of me at work	☐ 1	☐ 2	☐ 3	☐ 4	☐ 5
2	I can decide when to take a break	☐ 1	☐ 2	☐ 3	☐ 4	☐ 5
3	Different groups at work demand things from me that are hard to combine	☐ 1	☐ 2	☐ 3	☐ 4	☐ 5
4	I know how to go about getting my job done	☐ 1	☐ 2	☐ 3	☐ 4	☐ 5
5	I am subject to personal harassment in the form of unkind words or behaviour	☐ 1	☐ 2	☐ 3	☐ 4	☐ 5
6	I have unachievable deadlines	☐ 1	☐ 2	☐ 3	☐ 4	☐ 5
7	If work gets difficult, my colleagues will help me	☐ 1	☐ 2	☐ 3	☐ 4	☐ 5
8	I am given supportive feedback on the work I do	☐ 1	☐ 2	☐ 3	☐ 4	☐ 5
9	I have to work very intensively	☐ 1	☐ 2	☐ 3	☐ 4	☐ 5
10	I have a say in my own work speed	☐ 1	☐ 2	☐ 3	☐ 4	☐ 5
11	I am clear what my duties and responsibilities are	☐ 1	☐ 2	☐ 3	☐ 4	☐ 5
12	I have to neglect some tasks because I have too much to do	☐ 1	☐ 2	☐ 3	☐ 4	☐ 5
13	I am clear about the goals and objectives for my department	☐ 1	☐ 2	☐ 3	☐ 4	☐ 5
14	There is friction or anger between colleagues	☐ 1	☐ 2	☐ 3	☐ 4	☐ 5
15	I have a choice in deciding how I do my work	☐ 1	☐ 2	☐ 3	☐ 4	☐ 5
16	I am unable to take sufficient breaks	☐ 1	☐ 2	☐ 3	☐ 4	☐ 5
17	I understand how my work fits into the overall aim of the organisation	☐ 1	☐ 2	☐ 3	☐ 4	☐ 5
18	I am pressured to work long hours	☐ 1	☐ 2	☐ 3	☐ 4	☐ 5
19	I have a choice in deciding what I do at work	☐ 1	☐ 2	☐ 3	☐ 4	☐ 5

		Never	Seldom	Sometimes	Often	Always
20	I have to work very fast	☐ 1	☐ 2	☐ 3	☐ 4	☐ 5
21	I am subject to bullying at work	☐ 1	☐ 2	☐ 3	☐ 4	☐ 5
22	I have unrealistic time pressures	☐ 1	☐ 2	☐ 3	☐ 4	☐ 5
23	I can rely on my line manager to help me out with a work problem	☐ 1	☐ 2	☐ 3	☐ 4	☐ 5

		Strongly disagree	Disagree	Neutral	Agree	Strongly agree
24	I get help and support I need from colleagues	☐ 1	☐ 2	☐ 3	☐ 4	☐ 5
25	I have some say over the way I work	☐ 1	☐ 2	☐ 3	☐ 4	☐ 5
26	I have sufficient opportunities to question managers about change at work	☐ 1	☐ 2	☐ 3	☐ 4	☐ 5
27	I receive the respect at work I deserve from my colleagues	☐ 1	☐ 2	☐ 3	☐ 4	☐ 5
28	Staff are always consulted about change at work	☐ 1	☐ 2	☐ 3	☐ 4	☐ 5
29	I can talk to my line manager about something that has upset or annoyed me about work	☐ 1	☐ 2	☐ 3	☐ 4	☐ 5
30	My working time can be flexible	☐ 1	☐ 2	☐ 3	☐ 4	☐ 5
31	My colleagues are willing to listen to my work-related problems	☐ 1	☐ 2	☐ 3	☐ 4	☐ 5
32	When changes are made at work, I am clear how they will work out in practice	☐ 1	☐ 2	☐ 3	☐ 4	☐ 5
33	I am supported through emotionally demanding work	☐ 1	☐ 2	☐ 3	☐ 4	☐ 5
34	Relationships at work are strained	☐ 1	☐ 2	☐ 3	☐ 4	☐ 5
35	My line manager encourages me at work	☐ 1	☐ 2	☐ 3	☐ 4	☐ 5

Appendix 3: Action plan template and worked example

Action plan template

Standard area, eg Demands	Desired state	Current state	Practical solutions	Who will take the work forward?	When?	How will staff receive feedback?	Action completed?

Action plan template: An example using one element of Demands

Demands	Desired state	Current state	Practical solutions	Who will take the work forward?	When?	How will staff receive feedback?	Action completed?
The organisation provides employees with adequate and achievable demands in relation to the agreed hours of work	*Average to good performance*	*Bad/very bad performance* Workloads are not planned and peaks often occur during summer when people are on annual leave	1. Plan the work better and if peaks do clash with fixed annual leave commitments consider talking to other departments to see if temporary resources can be provided 2. Employees to talk to line managers about upcoming leave and potential difficulties with workload during monthly meetings	1. Line managers to lead and suggest the idea to senior managers 2. All, with line manager to lead	Issue to be raised at next senior managers meeting Immediately	1. Via monthly meetings, staff bulletins 2. During monthly meetings	Yes [Date] Yes – activity on-going

Appendix 4: Managing stress at work: A competency framework for line managers

Management competencies for preventing and reducing stress at work

Management Standard	Competency	Examples of positive manager behaviour	Examples of negative manager behaviour
Demands	Managing workload and resources	• bringing in additional resource to handle workload • aware of team members' ability • monitoring team workload • refusing to take on additional work when team is under pressure	• delegating work unequally to team • creating unrealistic deadlines • showing lack of awareness of how much pressure team are under • asking for tasks without checking workload first
Demands	Dealing with work problems	• following through problems on behalf of employees • developing action plans • breaking problems down into parts • dealing rationally with problems	• listening but not resolving problems • being indecisive about decisions • not taking problems seriously • assuming problems will sort themselves out
Demands	Process planning and organisation	• reviewing processes to see if work can be improved • asking themselves 'could this be done better?' • prioritising future workloads • working proactively	• not using consistent processes • sticking too rigidly to rules and procedures • panicking about deadlines rather than planning
Control	Empowerment	• trusting employees to do their work • giving employees responsibility • steering employees in a direction rather than imposing direction	• managing 'under a microscope' • extending so much authority employees feel a lack of direction • imposing 'my way is the only way'
Control	Participative approach	• provides opportunity to air views • provides regular team meetings • prepared to listen to employees • knows when to consult employees and when to make a decision	• not listening when employee asks for help • presenting a final solution • making decisions without consultation
Control	Development	• encourages staff to go on training courses • provides mentoring and coaching • regularly reviews development • helps employees to develop in role	• refuses requests for training • not providing upward mobility in the job • not allowing employees to use their new training

2

Management competencies for preventing and reducing stress at work (continued)

Management Standard	Competency	Examples of positive manager behaviour	Examples of negative manager behaviour
Support	Accessible/ visible	• communicating that employees can talk to them at any time • having an open-door policy • making time to talk to employees at their desks	• being constantly at meetings/away from desk • saying 'don't bother me now' • not attending lunches or social events
Support	Health and safety	• making sure everyone is safe • structuring risk assessments • ensuring all health and safety requirements are met	• not taking health and safety seriously • questioning the capability of an employee who has raised a safety issue
Support	Feedback	• praising good work • acknowledging employees' efforts • operating a no-blame culture passing positive feedback about the team to senior management	• not giving credit for hitting deadlines • seeing feedback as only 'one way' • giving feedback that employees are wrong just because their way of working is different
Support	Individual consideration	• provides regular one-to-ones • flexible when employees need time off • provides information on additional sources of support • regularly asks 'how are you?'	• assuming everyone is okay • badgering employees to tell them what is wrong • not giving enough notice of shift changes • no consideration of work–life balance
Relationships	Managing conflict	• listening objectively to both sides of the conflict • supporting and investigating incidents of abuse • dealing with conflict head on • following up on conflicts after resolution	• not addressing bullying • trying to keep the peace rather than sort out problems • taking sides • not taking employee complaints seriously
Relationships	Expressing and managing own emotions	• having a positive approach • acting calmly when under pressure • walking away when feeling unable to control emotion • apologising for poor behaviour	• passing on stress to employees • acting aggressively • losing temper with employees • being unpredictable in mood
Relationships	Acting with integrity	• keeps employee issues private and confidential • admits mistakes • treats all employees with same importance	• speaks about employees behind their backs • makes promises, then doesn't deliver • makes personal issues public

3

Management competencies for preventing and reducing stress at work (continued)

Management Standard	Competency	Examples of positive manager behaviour	Examples of negative manager behaviour
Relationships	Friendly style	• willing to have a laugh and a joke • socialises with team • brings in food and drinks for team • regularly has informal chats with employees	• criticises people in front of colleagues • pulls team up for talking/ laughing during working hours • uses harsh tone of voice when asking for things
Role and change	Communication	• keeps team informed of what is happening in the organisation • communicates clear goals and objectives • explains exactly what is required	• keeps people in the dark • holds meetings 'behind closed doors' • doesn't provide timely communication on organisational change
Other	Taking responsibility	• 'leading from the front' • steps in to help out when needed • communicating 'the buck stops with me' • deals with difficult customers on behalf of employees	• saying 'it's not my problem' • blaming the team if things go wrong • walking away from problems
Other	Knowledge of job	• able to put themselves in employees' shoes • has enough expertise to give good advice • knows what employees are doing	• doesn't have the necessary knowledge to do the job • doesn't take time to learn about the employee's job
Other	Empathy	• takes an interest in employees' personal lives • aware of different personalities and styles of working within the team • notices when a team member is behaving out of character	• insensitive to people's personal issues • refuses to believe someone is becoming stressed • maintains a distance from employees – 'us and them'
Other	Seeking advice	• seeks help from occupational health when necessary • seeks advice from other managers with more experience • uses HR when dealing with a problem	• n/a

4

References

1   *Psychosocial working conditions in Britain in 2007* HSE 2007 www.hse.gov.uk/statistics/pdf/pwc2007.pdf

2   *Self-reported work-related illness and workplace injuries in 2005/06: Results from the Labour Force Survey* HSE 2007 www.hse.gov.uk/statistics/lfs/lfs0506.pdf

3   *Development of internal company standards of good management practice and a task-based risk assessment tool for offshore work-related stressors* RR107 HSE Books 2003 ISBN 978 0 7176 2225 2 www.hse.gov.uk/research/rrhtm/index.htm

4   *Management of health and safety at work. Management of Health and Safety at Work Regulations 1999. Approved Code of Practice and guidance* L21 (Second edition) HSE Books 2000 ISBN 978 0 7176 2488 1

5   *Health and Safety at Work etc Act 1974 (c.37)* The Stationery Office 1974 ISBN 978 0 10 543774 1

6   *Safety representatives and safety committees* L87 (Third edition) HSE Books 1996 ISBN 978 0 7176 1220 8

7   *A guide to the Offshore Installations (Safety Representatives and Safety Committees) Regulations 1989. Guidance on Regulations* L110 (Second edition) HSE Books 1998 ISBN 978 0 7176 1549 0

8   *A guide to the Health and Safety (Consultation with Employees) Regulations 1996. Guidance on Regulations* L95 HSE Books 1996 ISBN 978 0 7176 1234 5

9   Mackay CJ, Cousins R, Kelly PJ, Lee S and McCaig RH (2004) '"Management Standards" and work-related stress in the UK: Policy background and science' *Work & Stress* **18** (2), 91-112

10 Cousins R, Mackay CJ, Clarke SD, Kelly C, Kelly PJ, and McCaig RH (2004) '"Management Standards" and work-related stress in the UK: Practical development' *Work & Stress* **18** (2), 113-136

11 *Five steps to risk assessment Leaflet* INDG163(rev2) HSE Books 2006 (single copy free or priced packs of 10 ISBN 978 0 7176 6189 3) www.hse.gov.uk/pubns/indg163.pdf

12 *Psychosocial working conditions in Great Britain in 2004* HSE 2004 www.hse.gov.uk/statistics/causdis/pwc2004.pdf

13 *Management competencies for preventing and reducing stress at work: Identifying and developing the management behaviours necessary to implement the HSE Management Standards* RR553 HSE Books 2007 www.hse.gov.uk/research/rrhtm/index.htm

Useful resources

If you would like to know more about HSC/E's work on managing the causes of work-related stress, contact HSE's Infoline on 0845 345 0055, e-mail: hse.infoline@natbrit.com or write to HSE Information Services, Caerphilly Business Park, Caerphilly CF83 3GG.

You can also visit HSE's stress web pages www.hse.gov.uk/stress where further resources are available.

The contact details below may be helpful for your own use or for using in any action plan you develop.

Mental health

Advice on all aspects of mental health is available from:

England

National Institute for Health and Clinical Excellence, MidCity Place, 71 High Holborn, London WC1V 6NA, Tel: 020 7067 5800, www.nice.org.uk

Scotland

Health Scotland, Woodburn House, Canaan Lane, Edinburgh EH10 4SG, Tel: 0131 536 5500, www.healthscotland.com

Wales

Welsh Assembly Government, Health and Social Services, Cathays Park, Cardiff CF10 3NQ, Tel: 0845 010 3300 (English) or 0845 010 4400 (Welsh), www.new.wales.gov.uk

For further information on helping people who are diagnosed with a mental illness contact:

MIND (National Association for Mental Health), 15-19 Broadway, London E15 4BQ, Mindinfoline: 0845 766 0163, www.mind.org.uk

Other sources of information on mental health include the following websites:

Charlie Waller Memorial Trust: www.cwmt.org

Depression Alliance: www.depressionalliance.org

Rethink Severe Mental Illness: www.rethink.org

The Samaritans: www.samaritans.org

Shift (as part of a Department of Health initiative) has produced a practical guide for managing and supporting people with mental health problems in the workplace: *Line managers' resource: A practical guide to managing and supporting people with mental health problems in the workplace* Shift 2007 http://shift.org.uk/~employers.html

If you do want to recruit a consultant to help you assess levels and sources of stress in your organisation, the British Psychological Society (BPS) can provide you with details of occupational psychologists and consultants:

BPS, St Andrews House, Leicester LE1 7DR, Tel: 0116 254 9568, www.bps.org.uk

Other sources of information on stress include the following websites:

International Stress Management Association: www.isma.org.uk

Developing Patient Partnerships: www.dpp.org.uk

Teacher Support Network: www.teachersupport.info

Equal opportunities

Employers' Forum on Disability, Nutmeg House, 60 Gainsford Street, London SE1 2NY, Tel: 020 7403 3020, www.employers-forum.co.uk

For further information on equal opportunities, racial equality and disability rights visit: www.equalityhumanrights.com

Disability Helpline (England) Tel: 08457 622 633 (Textphone 08457 622 644) or Freepost MID02164, Stratford-upon-Avon CV37 9BR

Equality and Human Rights Commission Helplines (for race, age, gender, sexual orientation, religion and belief and human rights):

England

Tel: 0845 604 6610 (Textphone 0845 604 6620) or Freepost RRLL-GHUX-CTRX, Arndale House, Arndale Centre, Manchester M4 3EQ

Wales

Tel: 0845 604 8810 (Textphone 0845 604 8820) or
3rd Floor, Capital Towers, Greyfriars Road,
Cardiff CF10 3AG

Scotland

Tel: 0845 604 5510 (Textphone 0845 604 5520) or
Freepost RRLL-GYLB-UJTA, The Optima Building, 58
Robertson Street, Glasgow G2 8DU

Counselling and stress management associations

British Association for Counselling and Psychotherapy,
BACP House, 15 St John's Business Park, Lutterworth
LE17 4HB, Tel: 0870 443 5252, www.counselling.co.uk

International Stress Management Association, PO Box 26,
South Petherton TA13 5WY, Tel: 07000 780430,
www.isma.org.uk

ISMA has produced the following leaflets which are also
available from HSE Books:

*Working together to reduce stress at work: A guide for
employees* Leaflet MISC686 International Stress
Management Association 2005 (single copy free or priced
packs of 15 ISBN 978 0 7176 6122 0)
www.hse.gov.uk/pubns/misc686.pdf

*Making the stress Management Standards work: How to
apply the Standards in your workplace* Leaflet MISC714
International Stress Management Association 2005 (single
copy free or priced packs of 15 ISBN 978 0 7176 6157 2)
www.hse.gov.uk/pubns/misc714.pdf

Work-life balance

For further information on work-life balance contact:

For employers in England and Scotland

Look at the BERR website at:
www.berr.gov.uk/employment/workandfamilies/flexible-
working/index.html

For employees in England and Scotland

Look at the Directgov website at:

www.direct.gov.uk/en/Employment/Employees/
WorkingHoursAndTimeOff/index.htm

See CIPD's factsheet on work-life balance in the working
time section of their website: www.cipd.co.uk/subjects

For employers in Wales

Welsh Assembly Government: www.wlbinwales.org.uk

Employment relations

For further information on trade union representation,
employee rights, and bullying and harassment at work,
contact:

TUC, Congress House, Great Russell Street, London
WC1B 3LS Tel: 020 7636 4030, www.tuc.org.uk

You may also find the following websites helpful:

Bully Online: www.bullyonline.org offers advice on the
symptoms of workplace bullying and how to tackle the
causes. It also features information on bullying in schools.

HSE website: www.hse.gov.uk/violence

The Andrea Adams Trust: www.andreaadamstrust.org – the
UK's only charity dedicated specifically to tackling workplace
bullying.

For further information on performance appraisal, personal
work plans, or managing attendance contact:

Chartered Institute of Personnel and Development,
151 The Broadway, London SW19 1JQ,
Tel: 020 8612 6200, www.cipd.co.uk

Information on Employee Assistance Programmes is
available from:

UK Employee Assistance Professionals Association,
3 Moors Close, Ducklington, Witney, Oxon OX29 7TW,
Tel: 0800 783 7616, www.eapa.org.uk

For further information and leaflets on employment rights,
good management practices, and bullying and harassment
at work, contact:

ACAS, Head Office, Brandon House, 180 Borough High
Street, London SE1 1LW, Helpline: 08457 47 47 47,
www.acas.org.uk

Further information

HSE priced and free publications are available by mail order from HSE Books, PO Box 1999, Sudbury, Suffolk CO10 2WA Tel: 01787 881165 Fax: 01787 313995 Website: www.hsebooks.co.uk (HSE priced publications are also available from bookshops and free leaflets can be downloaded from HSE's website: www.hse.gov.uk.)

For information about health and safety ring HSE's Infoline Tel: 0845 345 0055 Fax: 0845 408 9566 Textphone: 0845 408 9577 e-mail: hse.infoline@natbrit.com or write to HSE Information Services, Caerphilly Business Park, Caerphilly CF83 3GG.

Printed and published by the Health and Safety Executive   C100   11/07